THE MEN AT THE OFFICE

Working Women Talk About Working With Men

Edited by Cathy Feldman

CHESHIRE MEDICAL CENTER
DARTMOUTH-HITCHCOCK·KEENE

REBECCA B. OSBORNE
Organization Development Internal Consultant
HUMAN RESOURCES

580 – 590 Court Street
Keene, NH 03431
Tel: (603) 354-5454 Ext. 2479 • Fax: (603) 354-6519
Email: ROsborne@cheshire-med.com

BPB

Blue Point Books

Also from Cathy Feldman
Published by Blue Point Books

TWO YEARS WITHOUT SLEEP:
Working Moms Talk About Having a Baby and a Job

Library of Congress Catalog Number: 93-73061

ISBN 1-883423-02-03

Editor's Note:
All quotes not footnoted are from my interviews. A few of the
women quoted asked me not to use their real names.

INTRODUCTION

INTRODUCTION

The Men At The Office continues my series of books based on interviews with women in business. This time I asked women, "What is it like to work with men?" Their answers, sometimes hilarious, sometimes outrageous, are always right on target.

Again, as in *Two Years Without Sleep:* Working Moms Talk About Having A Baby And A Job, this new book combines the women's moving, perceptive quotes with facts and the advice of experts.

The many women who talked so freely to me about their experiences working with men share the hope that it will be a contribution to solving our problems in the work place. The more we learn to understand each other, the better our chances will be to build a better future for us all.

I thank the women who are making this series of books possible and dedicate these books to them.

CF

TABLE OF CONTENTS

The Interviews

BARBARA ABRAMS MINTZER, Management trainer and lecturer

LOUISE ANDRAS-RAMSEY, President, Paper Capers

MARSHA BAILEY, Executive Director, Women's Economic Ventures

DONNA BATES,* Human Resources Manager at a media company

IVY BERNHARDSON, Vice President, Senior Assoc. Counsel, General Mills

SHELLEY BOOKSPAN. Ph.D., President, PHR Environmental Consultants, Inc.

SUSAN CARTER,* Director of Human Resources with a Fortune 500 company

SHIRLEY CHERAMY, Managing Partner, Price Waterhouse, Los Angeles

LANI MEANLEY COLLINS, Counsellor at Law, Price, Postel & Parma

MARTHA CONNERS,* Benefits Manager with a Fortune 500 company

MARYANN CORRENTI, Partner, Arthur Andersen & Co., Dallas

JANE CRANE, Human Resources Manager with a large company

ANNE DAVIS,* Vice President with an international bank

CATHERINE DISHION, Owner, Santa Barbara Placement Agency

JOAN DZURO, Director of Human Resources with a newspaper

JOAN ENGSTROM, Senior Associate Counsel, General Mills

SANDRA EVERS-MANLY, Director of Diversity, Northrop Corp.

DEBRA FARRELL,* Vice President at a health service organiztion

ELLEN FRAZIER,* Vice President at a large financial institution

MARILYN GILBERT, Attorney at Law

PAT HEIM, Ph.D., Management and Organizational Consultant

KATHLEEN HARDY, Administrative Assistant, Public Works, County of Santa Barbara

NANCY HAWKS, Executive Director, Tri-County LEADS Clubs

JAN HILL, Owner, Hill Enterprises, a consulting firm

ANN JACKSON, President, Woodworkers Store

BEVERLY JAMES,* Vice President with a financial institution

ELLA KAYE,* Industrial Engineer

LORRAINE KENNEDY, Owner, Boss Graphics

LAURI LEIGHTY, Senior Vice President, Bank of Montecito

SHIRLEY LEMMEX, Contract Education, Santa Barbara City College

HELEN LINCOLN,* Sr. Vice President Finance with a large company

SARAH LITTON,* Partner in a major accounting firm

ELAINE MAHLA, Director, Workforce Partnership, DuPont-Merck

MARCIA MEIER, Editorial Page Editor with a newspaper

DIANA L. MEYERS, Public Relations and Fund Raising Consultant

PATRICIA MONTEMAYOR, County Affirmative Action Officer, Santa Barbara

CYNTHIA MORRIS, Partner, Price Waterhouse, Dallas

BETH NORTH,* Information Technology Specialist with a restaurant chain

KATHY ODELL, Chief Operating Officer, Medical Concepts Incorporated

BARBARA OTTO, Program Director, 9to5

DIANA PETERSON-MORE, Director, Human Resources, Times-Mirror Corporation

CHERI RAE, Editor and writer

CISSY ROSS, Business Editor with a newspaper

CATHERINE RUDDY, Partner, Adams, Duke & Haxeltine

GAIL SENECA, Managing Partner, Seneca Investment Fund

KATE SILSBURY, Financial Planner, IDS Financial Services, Inc.

LEILA SROUR, M.D., Pediatrics

RUTH TALBOT, Executive Vice President of a non-profit foundation

KAREN THOMPSON,* Senior executive with a Fortune 500 company

ANGIE UPHAM, Public Works Safety Officer, Santa Barbara Co.

TERRY WALKER, Management Consultant

SARI WEINER, President, SDW & Associates

ROSEMARY S. WHITNEY, Director, California Central Coast Region, Arthritis Foundation

CINDY WEBSTER, Management Trainer and Consultant, former fire captain

*Not their real names

WORKING WITH MEN

What Can a Woman Do?
Mrs. M. L. Rayne, 1885

Women's Work

"Forty-three or forty-four years ago Miss Harriet Martineau is reported to have said that, in Massachusetts, one of the most highly civilized and advanced communities in the world, there were but seven industries open to women who wanted to work. They might keep boarders, or set type, or teach needlework, or tend looms in cotton mills, or fold and stitch in book binderies.* This statement was rather too restrictive, because there were other forms of labor open to them, especially those of the needle. But there is no doubt that the opportunities of self-support for women by honest industry in some other way than that of domestic service were very few and very limited.

In the state of Massachusetts, which was the scene of Miss Martineau's reputed observation, it is now announced that there are two hundred and eighty-four occupations open to women, instead of seven, and that 251,158 women are earning their own living in these occupations, receiving from $150 to $3,000 every year. This computation does not include amateurs, or mothers and daughters in the household, and of course excludes domestic service."

*Counting folding and stitching as one each, this list adds up to only six occupations. There is no reference in the book to what Miss Martineau counted as the seventh.— Ed.

"I was taking three weeks off because I was getting married. My boss and I were talking about help during the time I was gone.

"I said, 'Well, if it was just somebody to answer the phone it would help.'

"He said, 'I don't understand why you can't check your voicemail while you're on your honeymoon.'

"Actually, he caught himself in the middle of the word *honeymoon* and changed the subject.

"Every day since then he told me, 'You will not pick up the phone and call in here while you're gone.'**"

—*Ellen Frazier*

MEN AND WOMEN
IN THE WORK FORCE

23% more women are employed in 1993 than in 1980

12% more men are employed in 1993 than in 1980 [1]

TOTAL MEN AND WOMEN EMPLOYED
1980 and 1993

In Millions

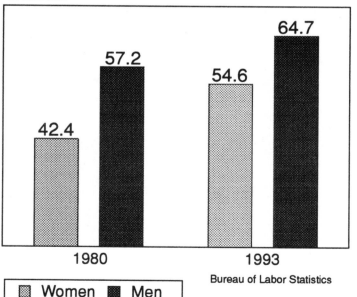

Bureau of Labor Statistics

1. Bureau of Labor Statistics

"A lot of women believe they'll get ahead if they just work hard and do their job.

"Men will take advantage of that. I know a number of women like that who feel they are actually in a preferred status because the men are so nice to them, when they are just being used.

"The men are perfectly happy to have a compliant worker bee who just works herself to death for them."

—Joan Engstrom

SURVEYS OF MEN AND WOMEN

WORKING WOMAN MAGAZINE ASKED WOMEN:

Do you think it is possible for women to make progress in your corporation faster now than five years ago?

33% of the women said yes in 1991

54% of the women said yes in 1985 [1]

THE YANKELOVICH MONITOR SURVEY

How men and women define masculinity:

". . .[T]he leading definition, ahead by a huge margin, has never changed. It isn't being a leader, athlete, Lothario, decision maker, or even just being "born male." It is simply this: being a 'good provider for his family.'"

— Susan Faludi [2]

How men and women define femininity:

"In 1992 we asked what femininity was, which we had never asked in the twenty-three years we've done this survey. The number one definition women gave was: 'balancing home, family, and a job.' Men's number one definition of femininity, ahead of all the others, was: 'sexually attractive to men.'"

— Susan Hayward, Yankelovich Partners [3]

1. Basia Hellwig, "Who Succeeds, Who Doesn't," *Working Woman,* November 1991

2. Susan Faludi, *Backlash,* Crown Publishers, Inc., 1991. Personal interview with Susan Hayward, Director, Yankelovich Partners

3. Susan Hayward, Director, Yankelovich Partners. Personal interview with the editor

"There was a seminar a few months ago about men and women in the workplace. They put the men in one room and the women in another, and asked them to write up attributes about how men view men, how men view women, and vise versa.

"One of the attributes frequently used to describe men that did not appear anywhere on the list describing women was *breadwinner*.

"The concept that women are not viewed as breadwinners inherently says women aren't committed to their careers. If men think that, we have a real tough problem."

—*Shirley Cheramy*

THERE ARE A LOT OF
WORKING MOMS

22.9 million working mothers in United States in 1993

8.8 million women in workforce with children 5 or younger [1]

THERE ARE A LOT OF WOMEN EXECUTIVES

95% increase in number of women in executive and managerial jobs between 1980 and 1990.

17% increase in number of men in executive and managerial jobs between 1980 and 1990. [2]

4.9 million women in executive, adminstrative and managerial positions in 1992 [1]

A 1992 SURVEY OF EXECUTIVE WOMEN

A survey of 400 top women executives in the nation's 1500 largest companies:

63% of senior women executives have children. [3]

---

1. Bureau of Labor Statistics
2. U.S. Census Bureau
3. Survey done by Korn/Ferry International and UCLA's John E. Anderson Graduate School of Management

MEN AND MOMS

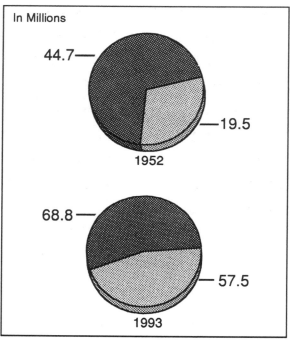

WOMEN IN THE WORK FORCE

1952 AND 1992

In Millions

44.7 —

—19.5

1952

68.8 —

— 57.5

1993

Bureau of Labor Statistics

■ Men   ▨ Women

The number of women in the work force has been growing steadily over the past 40 years. It has gotten to the point now where the overwhelming majority of women with children are working. Where's the day care at work? It's not there because management is still living in the 1950s when Mrs. Cleaver stayed at home to cook and clean for Ward, Wally, and the Beaver.[1]

---

1. William Lareau, *American Samaurai,* New Web Publishing Co, 1991

66 I started off basically being told that there was no reason to even write reviews of me because I would leave in two years. After a year, someone said, 'Oh, are you still here? I would have expected you to be married and pregnant by now.'

"An awful lot of women are told for so long, 'We don't expect you to stay. Why should we put you on the top clients when they expect continuity?' It becomes a self-fulfilling prophecy. 99

—Sarah Litton

WHAT MEN THINK ABOUT THEIR FAMILIES

80% of men said their families were very important [1]

"Men tend to imagine they are the only ones who have this work-family conflict. They feel kind of torn and feel that they are not doing right by their kids, and they want to do right by their kids, yet how can they if they're going to hold down a job and hold down their end of things at home?

"I think men resolve it by saying, 'I'm working for my family, so in a way, I'm contributing to my family by knocking myself out at work, by running to get the plane and stuff like that.'"

— Robert Weiss, research professor, University of Massachusetts, Boston [2]

PREGNANCY DISCRIMINATION

A survey of women graduates of Harvard's professional schools between the ages of 32 and 57:

Almost all of the 594 mothers in the group encountered discrimination from the moment they announced they were expecting.[3]

---

1. Men's Life Survey of 815 Men, Irene Lacher, "Bound for Glory," *Los Angeles Times,* October 21, 1990
2. *Los Angeles Times'* Survey of California men in July, 1990, Lacher, op.cit.
3. From a survey done by Deborah Swiss and Judith Walker, "Women and the Work/Family Dilemma," 1993

"There are double standards everywhere. If you are a woman and you have children in this organization, you are seen as somebody who can't give a hundred per cent. If you are man with children, you are seen as a stable worker."

— Ellen Frazier

"I really felt sorry for pregnant women on staff. The men acted like the women were constantly crabby and walked on eggshells around them. The women were absolutely fine. The men acted as if the women had lost their minds."

— Barbara Otto

"I was the first lawyer to be pregnant here. Nobody had tread on this ground before. I felt fine and I worked until the end. My boss was a nervous wreck near the end. The last couple weeks every time I'd go to the bathroom, if I was gone too long he'd start wandering around the area. He was afraid I'd go in the bathroom and have the baby."

— Ivy Bernhardson

“The president started treating me differently when I was pregnant. He wasn't consulting me on raises and on policy changes as he had been before. After about three or four weeks, I told him, 'I need to talk to you.' We went in the conference room and I shut the door. I said, 'You have been treating me differently. I know it's because I'm pregnant, and I know it's because you think I'm not going to come back and that you think you can't depend on me any more. That's bullshit. I'm going to come back.'

"He said, 'Honestly, I was not aware I was treating you any different.' I said, 'I don't care if you're not aware of it. It's not right, it's not fair, and I won't accept it.' He said, 'I'll be different.' And he was.”

—*Lauri Leighty*

"When I was adopting my baby, I went into my boss to tell him that I wanted to take a leave. I was ready for anything.

"The first question he said to me was, 'Are you going to nurse the baby?'

"I said, 'No, I don't think that is possible.'

"So he said, 'What do you need to stay home for?'

"That was the only time I ever cried. I walked down the hall in tears. After that he was very supportive. You never know what the reaction of management is going to be."

—*Helen Lincoln*

"One of my employees came in and told me she was pregnant. I got up and hugged her and kissed her and said, 'That is wonderful news. Tell me how you're feeling. Let's talk about it.'

"She started crying. She said, 'I was so afraid of what your reaction would be. So many people have horror stories about it.'

"That's sad. That is really sad. It's such a beautiful time, and they have to go through that."

—*Anne Davis*

IN AMERICA

PATERNITY LEAVE

1% of men take paternity leave [1]

MEN AS MOMS?

"New studies find that the behavior that we link to gender depends more on what an individual is doing and needs to do than on his or her biological sex. Sociologist Barbara Risman compared the personality traits of single father, single mother, and married parents. . . . Risman found that having responsibility for child care was as strongly related to 'feminine' traits, such as nurturance and sympathy, as being female was. The single men who were caring for children were more like mothers than like married fathers. These men were not an atypical group of especially nurturant men, either. They had custody of their children through circumstances beyond their control — widowhood, the wife's desertion, or the wife's lack of interest in shared custody."

— Carol Tavris [2]

1. From a study by Robert Half International reported by Amy Saltzman, "Trouble at the Top," *U.S. News & World Report*, June 17, 1991
2. Carol Tavris, *The Mismeasure of Woman*, Simon & Schuster, 1992

"There was this big meeting I had to come in for while I was on maternity leave. I brought the baby, but she started crying so I had to take her out and give her to my secretary. DeAnn is single, young, and doesn't know anything about babies.

"The baby wouldn't stop crying, and this guy in business development came in and said, 'Maybe it's the diapers.' So he and my secretary looked, and sure enough, it was the diapers. They didn't have any diapers in the outer office, and they didn't want to disturb me. All they could find was a cloth burping pad. They decided to put that on the baby, but they couldn't find any pins. The guy suggested, 'How about a stapler?' DeAnn was worried that maybe it would puncture the baby, so they took scotch tape and taped it around her in one continuous wrap.

"It was pretty funny when they showed me the baby wrapped in a burp pad with scotch tape."

—*Lauri Leighty*

WORKING TOGETHER

54.6 million women worked in 1993

64.9 million men worked in 1993 [1]

"Men and women . . . are not accustomed to being together day in and day out, as peers, so the taboos and rituals haven't been established."

—Dr. Helen Fisher, anthropologist, Museum of Natural History, New York City [2]

DURING THE CIVIL WAR

"When women were first leaving the farms during the Civil War to work in factories, there was a big debate in Congress. There was a big fear of allowing women to go to work in public places because of the possibility of them getting pregnant and not knowing who the father was."

—Marilyn Gilbert, attorney [3]

1. Bureau Labour Statistics
2. Nina J. Gaston, "I'm Not a Feminist, But..." *Los Angeles Times Magazine,* February 2, 1992
3. Marilyn Gilbert, Attorney at Law, Personal interview

OFFICE ROMANCE

OFFICE ROMANCE

According to a Gallup survey, 57 percent of American workers think office romances are "acceptable." But nobody asked if they thought they were a good idea.

Two categories of office romance:

Successful and tense. Lovers go to extraordinary lengths to keep their relationship secret. These relationships always end in marriage. Then, somebody eventually has to look for another job. Somebody is generally the wife.

Unsuccessful and tense. Lovers go to extraordinary lengths to keep their relationship secret, but the romance doesn't work out and everybody finds out anyway. Ultimately, somebody leaves. Usually the somebody is the woman.[1]

MISS MANNERS SAYS

What is it going to take to make people realize that formal manners must be reinstated in the work place? That the chummy atmosphere of first names, friendly retreats, office parties, background music and leisure clothing isn't working? It is Miss Manners' contention that the professional behavior should be strictly — well, professional.

The proper office demeanor is cordial, cheerful and helpful, but somewhat distant and impersonal. It has, of course, been argued that Miss Manners' system would end the human race, as the work place is now the chief venue people have to meet prospective mates.[2]

1. Gail Collins, "The Bold and The Unemployed," *Working Woman,* February 1993
2. Judith Martin, "Miss Manners," *Santa Barbara News Press*, December 16, 1991

"When I was an editor, I worked with these gorgeous, intelligent, creative guys who were completely inaccessible because I was the boss. I could hire them. I could run their photos and stuff. But there was no way I could date them. It was very difficult.

"At the first magazine I worked for, every guy the editor slept with ended up in the magazine. You always knew who her boyfriend was because the guys in the magazine would change. I never wanted to do that."

—Cheri Rae

"I met my husband, Tony, at the company we work for. I got pulled off a project because people knew that we were dating.

"The project was confidential, and Tony was on it. My boss told me that I couldn't be on the project because I was going out with Tony. They were concerned I was going to tell him something about it.

"I know that wouldn't have happened if it had been the other way around. That gives you a sense of their attitudes toward women, which is an automatic assessment that women aren't competent."

—Beth North

KEEP THAT SKIN COVERED

"Women tend to grab their necks when they are feeling insecure, during a debate or when they are challenged. Their skin gets blotchy, which can also be perceived as sexual excitement."[1]

"It's important not to show skin when working with the opposite sex." The more a woman's body is covered, the more respect men tend to feel toward her. Men are more likely to sexualize a woman, and therefore take her less seriously, if they see her skin. "To dress to get equal respect from men, you need to keep the flesh covered."

"There's no question, people respond emotionally before they respond intellectually, and we can use clothing as a tool to create the response we want."

— Jane Murdoch Miller, image consultant [2]

"Dress nonsexually. Don't send a sexual message. You can't sell your body and your brain at the same time."

— John T. Malloy, corporate consultant, author of *Dress for Success* [3]

1. Gaile Robinson, "The Politics of Appearance," *Los Angeles Times*, June 19, 1992
2. Andrea Heiman, "The Picture of Innocence?" *Los Angeles Times*, April 4, 1993
3. Trish Donnally, "Dressing for the Office," *San Francisco Chronicle*, January 20, 1992

❝I had a very awkward situation with a client early in my career. The client invited me out to dinner, and I didn't think it was really a business invitation. This was a major client, and I didn't know what to do.

"A woman partner told me to take control of the situation from the very start. She told me that if I remained in control, I would prevent the client from embarrassing himself. She said, 'Tell him, great, you're available, and that your husband and you would be delighted to take him out to dinner.'

"I did and it worked. And we've all become friends and stayed friends for a very long time.

"I was raised to let other people set the tone. When you realize you can set the tone, you can take control of the situation. It's amazing how well it works.❞

—*Catherine Ruddy*

THE FIRST NAME PARADOX

"Women are often caught in the grip of [a] paradox. They are far more often called by their first names and touched than are men. Talk show hosts, panel moderators, students, and others far more often address men with Ph.D.'s as 'Doctor' than they do women with Ph.D.'s. It's common for strangers — travel agents, salespeople, telephone order clerks — to use the first names of all women customers. In one sense, this shows condescension: lack of respect. Just as people feel free to touch, pat, and first-name children, they felt freer to use these friendly signs with women.

"But the fact remains that people who treat women in this way are doing it to be friendly; using 'Miss' or 'Mrs.' (let alone, 'Ms.'!) would feel awkward, like anything that goes against habit. Many women prefer to be called by first name because it is distancing to be addressed by title-last name. And women are more likely than men to be troubled by distancing."

— Deborah Tanen [1]

1. Deborah Tannen, Ph.D., *That's Not What I Meant!*, Ballantine Books, 1986

"I have what I call my corporate bathing suit. It is the ugliest bathing suit you have ever seen. I take it along whenever I go to people's homes or a manager's meeting at a corporate retreat in case one of the men says, 'Donna, why don't you come and have drinks with us in the hot tub?' I'm not in the position, as a senior management person, to say no."

—Donna Bates

A TRUE OR FALSE QUIZ
ABOUT PLATONIC RELATIONSHIPS

1. Older people are more apt than younger people to have close platonic friendships.

FALSE - Younger people today tend to have more opposite sex friendships. In the past, such friendships often were considered taboo. It was assumed unlikely that one would have a close friendship with someone of the opposite sex that was strictly platonic.

2. Platonic friendships are growing in this country.

TRUE - Men and women are beginning to relate to each other as individuals rather than merely as sex objects, and that has helped open the door for platonic relationships. In most colleges today, men and women relate as people first, especially when they share co-ed living quarters — which makes non-sexual friendship between the sexes seem natural and normal.

3. What friendship means and what one expects of friendship are basically the same for people regardless of gender.

FALSE - Males and females tend to view friendship somewhat differently. Trust, confidentiality and the sharing of intimacy are much more important to females, whereas males are likely to emphasize doing things together, such as sports, or the pleasure they find in each other's company.[1]

---

1. Dr. Joyce Brothers, "Putting Friendships Up for Examination," *Los Angeles Times*, December 23, 1992

"I worked for a man who had a very jealous wife. She used to call our secretary all the time and tell her to keep an eye on me because she knew I was 'trying to make partner any way I could.' Our secretary kept reporting all these little conversations.

"Finally I said, 'The next time she says that, tell her that if I were looking for power, there are much more powerful men than her husband. If I were looking for money, there are much richer men than her husband. If I were looking for looks, there are much better looking men than her husband. As it is, I'm happily married, so I'm not looking for any of the three.'

"I don't know if that message was ever delivered, but I think it was. His wife has hated me ever since."

—*Sarah Litton*

"Women have become so powerful that our independence has been lost in our own homes and is now being trampled and stamped underfoot in public."

— Cato, 195 B.C.

MALE FEARS

DEPRESSION BACKLASH

At intervals since 1920, there have been loud and somewhat acrimonious demands for women to "get back into the home—where they belong." During the Depression a few large corporations announced a change in policy regarding women and fired all women holding executive positions, replacing them with men. Some even dismissed their feminine clerks and stenographers and engaged boys and young men to take their places. For a time it seemed as if the calendar were going to be moved back a few decades and women would be obliged to buy washboards or sewing machines in order to earn a living.[1]

A GALLUP POLL ASKING SHOULD MARRIED WOMEN WORK:

82% opposed married women working in 1936

[In the late 1930s], bills [were] introduced in the legislatures of twenty-six states against married women workers. Only one of those passed. This was in Louisiana, and it was later repealed. Six other states have either joint resolutions or governors' orders restricting married women's right to work. Three other states have made a practice of prohibiting married women from working in public employment. . . .[2]

---

1. Doree Smedley and Lura Robinson, *Careers in Business for Women*, E.P. Dutton & Company, Inc., 1945
2. Ruth Shallcross, "Shall Married Women Work?" For the National Federation of Business and Professional Women's Clubs, Public Affairs Pamphlet No. 40, New York, 1941

66 L ately women have been telling me there is a backlash they haven't felt in a long time. There is a very hostile environment right now compared to how it was. I think it's resentment.

"Some of the women were talking about leaving their present assignments, but we started comparing notes, and they realized that it wasn't going to be better anywhere else.

"One of the women is a partner in a law firm, and she is married to a doctor. She said the other partners in her law firm hate it because she has more money than they do. 99

—Joan Engstrom

IN AMERICA

American women represent two thirds of all poor adults and face the worst gender-based pay gap in the world.

80% of full-time working women make less than $20,000 per year [1]

IN THE WORLD

50% of the world's population are women

70% of world's work is done by women

45% of world's food is produced by women

10% of world's income is held by women

1% of world's property is owned by women [2]

"[M]en won't easily give up a system in which half the world's population works for next to nothing, . . .[and] precisely because that half works for so little, it may have no energy left to fight for anything else."

— Marilyn Waring, economist [3]

1. U.S. Bureau of Census
2. Humphrey Institute of Public Affairs, University of Minnesota, "Looking to the Future: Equal Partnership Between Men and Women in the 21st Century."
3. Naomi Wolf, *The Beauty Myth,* William Morrow and Co., 1991

6 6 I grew up expecting if I did a good job I would get a raise. When I got out in the real world, it was the opposite. They were going to pay you as little as possible.

I had one boss I asked for a raise. Instead of giving me a raise, he tore me apart. He gave me this completely negative review, and then sent me flowers. 9 9

— Marsha Bailey

6 6 Women are totally different from men because women are so relationship based. They will take time out to work as a team. They will take time out for a colleague who's in distress.

"What women bring to business is not validated as much because it can't be identified like the bottom line on a financial statement. Without those women the bottom line on the financial statement would not be as good, but how do you measure what impact they have? And how do you reward it? If you can't measure it, you can't reward it. 9 9

— Shirley Lemmex

THE NARROWING WAGE GAP

WOMEN'S WEEKLY EARNINGS COMPARED TO MEN'S:

Year	Men	Women
1980	$358	$215
1990	$497	$368
1993	$514	$395

In 1980: Women earned **60 cents** for every dollar men earned.

In 1993: Women earned **77 cents** for every dollar men earned.[1]

WOMEN ARE EARNING MORE BUT . . .

"When you look at the figures for women in the median-pay bracket, the narrowing of the gap in the 80s was about 75 percent due to men's wages falling, not female wage growth."

— Jared Bernstein, Economic Policy Institute, Washington, D.C.[2]

---

1. Bureau of Labor Statistics
2. Jared Bernstein, Economic Policy Institute, Washington, D.C.

" A firm I worked for was looking for an office manager. They'd had two men, both alcoholics, whom they'd had trouble with. Both had left with huge bills that they didn't pay.

"The firm had an application from a woman who was an assistant manager at one of the major firms in Denver. The men at the meeting said, 'It would be good to get a woman. We could get her for less money.' "

—Ruth Talbot

" I gave a talk to the downtown Rotary. At that time it was all men. My topic was, 'The Joy of Working, Not Cooking.'

"After I finished giving my speech about women who had successful careers, the main thing the men wanted to know was why the women were paid so much. "

—Patricia Montemayor

LIGHTEN UP!

"Oh, lighten up, already. This whole term 'male-bashing'— if women did it for 30 years, we still wouldn't even the score. I say, learn to laugh at yourself, like women have had to over the years. Develop a sense of humor. Or at least marry one."

— Diane Ford, comedian, at a comedy
benefit for National Coalition against
Sexual Assault [1]

57.3% of all women worked in 1992.[2]

"The idea that the white women of America will join an alliance to bring down white men is so hilarious that it could only have been thought up on a university campus. In the academic world, women are viewed as a separate power group, abused by a relentlessly rape-minded and harassing masculinist oppressor. In the real world, most women want equality, good jobs and families, not front-line action in a war to topple their husbands, brothers and sons."

— John Leo, columnist [3]

---

1. Nancy Wride, "Man, Can't you Take a Joke?" *Los Angeles Times*, September 26, 1992
2. Bureau of Labor Statistics
3. John Leo, "Dangerous Race-Gender Myths," United Press Syndicate, April 21, 1993

"There's a lot of concern and fear among white males these days about women moving up. Women need to be sensitive to that. One man told me, 'I'm not afraid of women. But I'm afraid if I let go of the power, I'm going to get paid back for all the wrongs ever done to them by any man they've ever worked for.'

"To me it's an irrational fear. They're just going to have to face stiffer competition."

—*Joan Dzuro*

EQUAL EMPLOYMENT OPPORTUNITIES COMMISSION SEXUAL HARASSMENT CHARGES, 1993:[1]

12,368

ILLEGAL SEXUAL HARASSMENT

Four categories:

1. Quid Pro Quo: something is given in return for something else, as when a supervisor makes unwelcome sexual advances and either states or implies the victim must submit to keep her job or get a raise.

2. Hostile environment: even if no threat is involved, things like sexually explicit jokes, pinups, graffiti, vulgar statements, abusive language, innuendoes, and overt sexual conduct can create a hostile environment.

3. Sexual favoritism: when a supervisor rewards only those employees who submit to sexual demands, other employees can claim they are penalized by the sexual attention directed at the favored coworkers.

4. Harassment by nonemployees: an employer can be held responsible for harassment by people outside the company like customers or vendors if the employer has control or could have control over their actions.[2]

1. Equal Employment Opportunities Commission. According to the EEOC, this is the highest number of charges ever filed.
2. Ellen Bravo and Ellen Cassedy, *The 9to5 Guide to Combating Sexual Harassment,* John Wiley & Sons, Inc., 1992

SEXUAL HARASSMENT STORIES

SEXUAL HARASSMENT IN THE CITY OF LOS ANGELES, 1992

37% of the 4,887 female employees of the city who responded to the survey said they have been harassed on the job

2% of the women have lodged complaints.[1]

LOS ANGELES, JANUARY 13, 1993:

Los Angeles Police Chief Willie L. Williams has called for development of a department-wide training program on sexual harassment that for the first time would include LAPD's top brass, including Williams himself.

"This would be the first time ever members of the department who are the rank of captain and above will be required to receive training about this issue."

— Jennifer McKenna, managing director
of California Women's Law Center [2]

---

1. Report from the Commission on the Status of Women, City of Los Angeles, 1993
2. John L. Mitchell, "Williams Plans Training for Top Brass on Harassment Issue," *Los Angeles Times*, January 13, 1993

"In the 15 years I've been in Human Resources, the main complaint has been harassment. Fifteen years ago we didn't call it that. It was just something that your boss did."

—Joan Dzuro

A SURVEY OF WOMEN ABOUT MEN

Have most men in the United States become more understanding about the issues that concern you?

27% Yes
68% No

Have bosses become more sensitive to sexual harassment problems?

66% Yes [1]

THE COMPLIMENT ISSUE

"If personal criticism is objectionable, then why aren't personal compliments charming? Because no employee should be subject to personal appraisal from a boss, even if the judgment is favorable. Proper compliments have to do with job performance, and the best of all are the ones that go into the paycheck or on the record."

— Miss Manners [2]

"When the men run around and ring their hands and say, 'Now I don't know what to do,' somehow I'm not losing sleep over their anguish. When in doubt, don't do it! Is this really hard to wrap your mind around? If you think it might hurt somebody's feelings or make somebody uncomfortable, don't do it!"

— Robin Moore, Editor, *Ms.* Magazine

1. Newsweek Poll conducted December 17-18, 1992, *Newsweek*, December 28, 1992
2. Miss Manners/Judith Martin, "Bosses Fall behind on Etiquette," *Los Angeles Times,* May 6, 1990

66 **W**e had a fairly verbally abusive harasser at a senior level who called down to my office and told me to get my ass up there.

"I said, 'Well, sweetheart, do you want just my ass or can all of me come?'

"I went to his office and he was sitting there reeling from this piece of insubordination. I said, 'Sweetheart, not even my husband calls it my ass.' He didn't mess with me after that.

"Several women on my level came to me and said, 'You're stronger than us. We need him to get off our case.' I said, 'I think each one of you has to tackle your own problems. I think you have a responsibility to do that for yourself.'

"One of them chose to leave as a result of that." 99

—*Debra Farrell*

WHY SOME MEN RESENT SEXUAL HARASSMENT POLICIES

Sexual harassment policies are sometimes viewed as a giant step backward, toward the days when behavior and speech were monitored by a powerful female figure. "If you use those nasty words, I'll wash out your mouth with soap."

Workplace policies that seem to dictate what they can and cannot say often create the same resentment and angry rejection that a mother treating her adult son like a 5-year-old would.

— Cindy Webster, management
consultant [1]

Too many men still "don't get it." But as the dust settles, most Americans — women nearly as much as men — are likely to back away from the more radical demands that women be granted an individual right to define all encounters between women and men.

Too many women have fathers, brothers, husbands or lovers who could be destroyed by false accusations. Too many women know that women may behave ambiguously — if only because, having been raised in what remains a sexually unequal world, they have been encouraged to please those more powerful and, in attempting to please, can get drawn into compromising situations.

— Elizabeth Fox Genovese, professor
of Humanities [2]

1. Cindy Webster, "Facing off on sexual harassment," *Fire Chief,* August, 1992
2. Elizabeth Fox-Genovese, Eleanore Raoul Professor of Humanities at Emory University, "Women Gain In Quest for Enhanced Dignity," *Santa Barbara News Press,* January 6, 1992

"One of the guys in our office made the comment, 'It's not fun any more. You can't tell jokes any more.' I said, 'You can tell jokes, but you've got to be careful who you tell the joke to and who's around. You wouldn't be standing in an ethnically mixed group and start telling some obnoxious joke. It may not be fun any more but what you've got to understand is that it hasn't been fun for a lot of these women who've been standing around all these years hearing this stuff.'"

—*Shirley Cheramy*

"This guy in my office borrowed ten dollars from me. He came in the next day and, in front of the whole office, said, 'Thanks, it was lots of fun. I'll tell all my friends about you.' He thought he was being really funny."

—*Kathleen Hardy*

"One company I worked at had a woman in a manufacturing area who did something very interesting. There were girlie pictures on all the men's tool boxes and lockers. This was before that type of thing was under sexual harassment. I was the human resource manager, and she came in and complained. I said, 'We could make them take the pictures down, which will make them angry at you. Or we could try to think of something else.' She said, 'How about if I bring in some men's pictures?' It wasn't my favorite idea, but since there were no rules and regulations at the time, I said, 'That's fine. Let's see what happens.'

"The pictures she brought were partially clothed men and one nude from the back, nothing like what you'd consider pornography. She put them on her tool box and locker, the same places the men had their girlie pictures. The men went nuts. They were infuriated that she would put up these disgusting pictures of men. A group of them came to me and said they wanted the pictures taken down.

"I said, 'Look, guys. We can do one of two things. Either you all get to keep your pictures, because she has every right to keep the same type of pictures you do. Or you can all get rid of them.' They voted to get rid of them."

—*Joan Dzuro*

" **A** t one of the magazines I worked for, the ad rep didn't wear any underwear. He always wore loose shorts and would put his legs up on the table and call you into his office. We were on equal footing. He was the ad guy; I was the editor. He would sit there with his balls hanging out and say normal stuff.

"It was kind of shameful. It's the kind of thing like when you're a kid and see someone exposing himself, you feel like it's your fault.

"I didn't know who to tell or what to say. It was so embarrassing, and he was so obnoxious about it. I know he did it to other people. I was young and cute and still played those flirty games. I think there was this sense that he liked me, even though it was very weird.

"And what if I had done something? It was definitely the boys' network. This was one of the guys who went surfing with the publisher every day. "

—Cheri Rae

"My boss was giving me a lot of trouble, pulling the kind of things that could bring on a lawsuit.

"I went to the managing partners and said, 'I'm not going to be the one to sue. Anybody who brings a harassment suit in this day and age is not going to have a career. But someday somebody is going to prefer a settlement to a career, and you guys really ought to get your act together.'

"Going over the heads of narrow-minded people can be very career-limiting if you don't succeed.

"Fortunately the partners believed me. After that, the man who was giving me a hard time got very polite.

"But don't expect the problems to stop when you move up. You need a lot of patience and a sense of humor. When I was one level below partner, we had a partner who would come into my office late at night and proposition me. He made pretty blatant comments. He'd say, 'I've decided you can have me if you want me this evening.' I'd say, 'I'm much too overworked to consider that.' Once he said he would have to get very wealthy because if I was ever single again, he was sure I would be very expensive. I told him that he would never make that much money in his entire life.

"He pulled the same sort of stuff on one of my friends. She was trying to get an advance on her bonus by a week. He sort of offered to advance her bonus if she would do some favors for him, and he was fairly explicit. He also put cute little notes like that in writing and she kept them in a file. She handed the file over to the national managing partner, and this guy lost his position because of harassment charges."

—*Sarah Litton*

"These two guys were always grabbing the rear ends of secretaries who walked by, or as a woman who was well-endowed came toward one of them, they'd put their hands out like two basketballs. They'd pretend to grab your breasts too.

"The men felt they could do it with impunity because they had higher rank than most of the women. I was getting a little of that harassment, but the men were frustrated because I wasn't reacting the way they wanted. The other women in the department were getting a lot worse. I'd say, 'Why don't you tell someone?' And they said, 'Bev, I have a little girl to support. I can't afford to lose the job.'

"I sued because I couldn't stand what was going on. I said to my husband, 'Look, I can find another job. It's worth it to me.' So I put up the money and got a lawyer who cost me $5,000. The bank was very surprised. Here I was, a vice-president, and I was suing them. They dragged it out as long as they could but they weren't going to let it go to trial.

"The two men were fired. My complaints were that the women were being harassed and discriminated against as far as pay. Every woman in our department got a raise.

"I stayed for seven years after that. I was like the plague. I could have died in my chair. Eventually they had to make me manager. They had no choice; I was doing a good job and had earned it. They wouldn't have done anything unless they had to."

—*Beverly James*

66"Women are so sensitive now we think everything is gender or we think everything is race, and it isn't. Not everything has some hidden meaning.

"I've talked to men who've said even the small talk before a meeting makes them uneasy because there has been so much in the work place about sexual harassment, they don't want there to be any hint that they have a personal attraction or anything personal about anything they are saying.

"There is lots of fear about anything they say or an innocent touch, in fact even shaking hands. Many of them are reluctant to shake women's hands. I've been having a series of meetings with an outside consultant every few weeks. He'd shake the hand of all the men in the room. I was the only female and he would never shake my hand. About a month ago I went up to him and said, 'Won't you shake my hand?' Now he shakes my hand.99

—*Susan Carter*

"When I started working at my present job, the division manager had an administrative assistant take me aside and tell me that sexual harassment and discrimination were not to be tolerated. If I ever had a problem I should report it right away. It was such a refreshing attitude, I couldn't believe it. I just stood there with my mouth open. One of the reasons I came to work in this department was because of the problems I'd had at my previous job. I married that division manager. I figured he was my kind of guy."

—Angie Upham

WHEN ALL ELSE FAILS, WE YELL

When people can't understand what we're trying to say, what do we do? We say it again — louder. And if we still aren't getting the point across, we say it even LOUDER. And if we sense that the communication breakdown is total, we go all out and also repeat the words more slowly.

THREE WAYS TO GET THE MESSAGE ACROSS BETTER

- Best Method: Alter the content of the message
- Next best method: Alter the details of the message
- Worst method: Alter the speech. Almost everybody starts with this method. Not only doesn't it get the message across any better, shouting also tends to raise our blood pressure.[1]

---

1. Study done by Charles R. Bergen, Ph.D. Professor of rhetoric and communication, USC Davis in *Psychology Today,* November/December 1992

FROM YELLING
TO OUTRAGEOUS

UNCOUTH BEHAVIOR

Men's outbursts often spring from their "sense of entitlement" — the belief that they deserve, for instance, courteous service from a hotel desk clerk after a long business trip.

For women, a tantrum is more likely to be frustration . . . . A woman might throw a tantrum, for instance, after repeatedly asking her boss for a raise and not getting one.

— Lee Ann Clark, assoc. professor of
Psychology, Southern Methodist Univ. [1]

—∞— 1885 —∞—

The twenty-seventh annual commencement of the Pennsylvania College of Dental Surgery was held at the Academy of Music, Philadelphia. Of the fifty-nine graduates, five were ladies, all of whom ranked among the ten highest students of the class. . . . It is considered that the presence of these ladies has been of great advantage to the character of the class, as the uncouth element formerly obtaining in medical schools has been entirely subdued by their presence.

— Mrs. M. L. Rayne, author [2]

1. Kathleen Doheny, "Temper, Temper!", *Los Angeles Times,* September 3, 1991
2. Mrs. M. L. Rayne, *What Can a Woman Do?* F.B. Dickerson & Co., 1885

66 **I**t's amazing how the men treat each other. If they have a conflict, they can sit in a meeting and rip each other apart and twenty minutes later walk out and say, 'Hey, you want to have lunch?'

"Women take things much more personally. 99

—Donna Bates

AGGRAVATION

2.5X

Men are two and a half times more likely than women to be aggravated by their bosses or colleagues.[1]

FOR WOMEN ONLY

"The truth is many women need an opportunity to develop competence and confidence without the pressures and even well-meant protections that men often provide.

"In sailing we found that women's way of learning is different from men's — more global, with a lot more explanation and hands-on demonstration. Womanship's motto is, 'Nobody yells'."

— Suzanne Pogell, president of
Womanship, a sailing school [2]

1. Opinion Research Corporation in survey of over 2,000 employees, *Working Woman,* September 1992
2. Judi Dash, "`For Women Only' Trips Are Gaining Converts," *Los Angeles Times,* April 18, 1993

❝ A t a seminar on how men and women view each other, one of the attributes frequently listed for women was *Emotional*. A woman in the room said, 'Oh, you mean like somebody gets up and yells and screams and throws a temper tantrum. Is that what you mean by emotional?'

She was obviously describing male behavior. All these guys suddenly got this enlightened look on their faces, like, gee, we never thought of it like that. ❞

—Shirley Cheramy

WHY WE CRY

Eighty-five percent of women and 73 percent of men reported that they felt better after they cried, in a study done by biochemist William H. Frey II, Ph.D., research director of the Dry Eye and Tear Research Center, St. Paul, Minnesota.

"Tears may literally help cleanse our bodies; they play an important biological role in reducing stress. Since we know that stress can aggravate all kinds of conditions, from ulcers to hypertension, even colitis, it may be a mistake not to cry."

Women cry four times more often than males. Possible biological explanation: Women produce more prolactin — a hormone that promotes tears — and have larger tear glands. It could also be cultural.

"Boys are taught at an early age that to cry is a loss of control, that male crying is bad."

— William H. Frey II, Ph.D.[1]

---

1. Nancy Stesin, "The Best Stress Relief," *Ladies Home Journal*, July 1992

"I've seen a vice-president of a company get angry, rip the phone out of the wall and storm out of a meeting he was conducting. Everybody just sat there silent and fiddled with things knowing he'd come back. He came back a half hour later and then the meeting went on. That's being a man.

"If a woman had done that, she would have had no credibility whatsoever. Men can basically say and do whatever they want and be angry. However, if a woman shows any kind of emotion whatsoever, she's condemned as too emotional. Especially crying. Crying is a death knell.

"When people try to make a big thing out of crying, I say, 'So? Would you rather she hauled off and punched your lights out? That's how women express their anger. Instead of beating on your desk or throwing something, they're going to sit there and cry because they are so upset. That's just a natural release for women. Hand her a tissue, and when she calms down you'll talk. Just like with a man, you give him a punching bag, and when he calms down you'll talk.'"

—*Joan Dzuro*

DESCRIBING MEN, DESCRIBING WOMEN

PUTTING THE SHOE ON THE OTHER FOOT

(Excerpted from *Science Magazine*, October 26, 1982) "...the female brain was well-lateralized — that is, manifests less hemispheric specialization — than the male brain for visuospatial functions."

"Notice the language," Carol Tavris writes. "The female brain is 'less specialized' than, and by implication inferior to, the male brain. [He] did not say that the female brain was 'more integrated' than the male's."[1]

GRAVE INJUSTICE

Men and women who hold the same job while alive are often perceived very differently after they die. From a comparison of obituaries published in four European newspapers in 1974, 1980, and 1986:

Men were:	Women were:
• intelligent	• adorable
• indefatigable	• faithful
• experienced	• likable
• entrepreneurial	• courageous [2]

---

1. Carol Tavris, *The Mismeasure of Woman,* Simon & Schuster, 1992
2. Psychologist Erich Kirchler of the Johannes Kepler University in Linz, Austria. *Psychology Today,* May/June, 1993

"In rookie academy training to be a firefighter, we had exercises where your group had to decide what to do in a rescue situation. I would give a suggestion, and the men would ignore it. A male rookie would say exactly the same thing and they'd jump on it. I called them on it. I said, 'Wait a minute. I just suggested that. Why don't you respond to my suggestion?' One of them looked at me and said, 'We'll be damned if we'll do what a woman tells us.'

"That noon hour, I went out running. I was crying because I was so frustrated. But when you're running, you come back flushed and red and sweaty, so nobody knew the difference. They just thought it was sweat.

"I walked back to the station feeling really down, but I wanted to hang in there. When I walked in one of the firefighters said to me, 'We want to trade you. We want you instead of our girl firefighter because she's always crying, and you never cry.'"

—*Cindy Webster*

EMOTIONS, EMOTIONS, EMOTIONS

If women often avoid confrontations with men because they subconsciously fear violence, many men avoid face-offs with women because they fear an emotional outburst, especially tears. Not only do men not know how to respond to such a situation, they tend to resent it. The bottom line: Extreme emotions of any kind, including anger, are off-limits.[1]

HOW HARD ARE MANAGERS WORKING?

95% work more than a 40-hour workweek

49% vacationed only two weeks in the past twelve months

66% said their jobs are more stressful than they were a decade ago [2]

"A lot of times you just stop worrying when you get older. This has a lot to do with the degree to which you can tolerate uncertainty. As you get wiser, you can tolerate uncertainty. And for some people, once something really bad happens to them, they quit worrying. All of a sudden they decide not to worry any more. It puts things in perspective."

— Dr. Gary Emery, director of Los Angeles Center for Cognitive Therapy[3]

1. Adele Scheele, Ph.D., "Confronting Your Boss," *Working Woman,* May 1993
2. Priority Management Systems, Inc, "The 21st Century Workplace," *Newsweek,* June 11. 1990
3. Shari Roan, "Oh, No! Now What Could Go Wrong?" *Los Angeles Times,* March 30, 1993

❝**O**ne of the things I do, it's almost a fault that I'm trying to get over, is that I react very calmly to anything that comes up. I'm very good at being very cool and being very careful about what I say. Afterwards I really get upset and I'll be up all night long just thinking about the situation.❞

—Marcia Meier

❝**I**'ve been told by many men that I am more like dealing with a business man than most business men they know. I could be insulted by that. I could be flattered. But I think the only reason that is the case is because I am able to maintain what appears to be a calm and almost detached demeanor because of the bio-feedback training I've had.

"What I do now when a difficult situation arises is think, have I done something to particularly annoy him. Usually not. When you realize this, it doesn't trigger a guilt reaction, and over time, it helps increase your self-esteem because you become more in control of your life.❞

—Diana L. Meyers

" I was having dinner with a senior member of management, he looked at me and said, 'Don't you ever swear?'

"I said, 'Excuse me?'

'Don't you ever swear?'

"I said, 'No, not really.'

"He said to me, 'You need to swear more. People will take you more seriously.'

"So I tried it. And every time I want to make a point at a meeting, I swear, and it works. "

—*Donna Bates*

"Men say outrageous things. A lot depends on the source. It's entirely different when a guy you trust says something than when it comes from a guy you distrust.

"A woman who's a corporate controller told me a story: She recently had braces, which was a very difficult decision for her. A high level executive in the company said to her, 'Now, Ruth, does it impede oral sex?'

"That's the kind of guy he is. After she finished laughing, she said, 'Well, as a matter of fact, Mike, yes it does.'

"Those are the kinds of things women have to put up with. But again, maybe men do also because maybe men say that to each other. I think half the time they do it to see how far they can push. It's part of seeing if you're going to act like a white male and be part of their group."

—*Helen Lincoln*

ROSIE THE RIVETER

. . . [A] wartime economy opened millions of high-paying industrial jobs to women, and the government even began to offer minimal day care and household assistance. Federal brochures saluted the hardy working woman as a true patriot. Strong women became cultural icons; Rosie the Riveter was revered and, in 1941, Wonder Woman was introduced. Women welcomed their new economic status; 5 to 6 million poured into the work force during the war years, 2 million into heavy-industry jobs; by the war's end, they would represent a record 57 percent of all employed people. Seventy-five percent reported in government surveys that they were going to keep their jobs after the war — and, in the younger generation, 88 percent of the 33,000 girls polled in a Senior Scholastic survey said they wanted a career, too. . . .

But with the close of World War II, efforts by industry, government, and the media converged to force a female retreat. Two months after a U.S. victory had been declared abroad, women were losing their economic beachhead as 800,000 were fired from the aircraft industry; by the end of the year, 2 million female workers had been purged from heavy industry. Employers revived prohibitions against hiring married women or imposed caps on female workers' salaries; and the federal government proposed giving unemployment assistance only to men, shut down its day care services, and defended the "right" of veterans to displace working women.

—Susan Faludi, author [1]

---

1. Susan Faludi, *Backlash,* Crown Publishers, Inc., 1991

THE OFFICE MEN'S CLUB

GOING TO LUNCH WITH MEN

WHAT'S IN

- Open doors for men. Whoever gets to the door first should open it.
- Women should stand when introduced just like a man.
- Wait until coffee is served to talk business during a business lunch, unless your guest brings the subject up before.[1]

GOING TO JAPAN?

- If possible, when you are traveling solo, find a female colleague or translator to accompany you. A man may be mistaken as your superior.
- In a meeting, never take a seat near the door — you might be mistaken for administrative help.
- Don't let yourself be entertained by the "office ladies" at a Japanese firm. These women are not your colleagues. Graciously decline and offer an alternative.
- Don't slurp your soup or noodles even if the men do. It is impolite for a woman.[2]

---

1. Syndi Seid, founder of Advanced Etiquette, San Francisco in article by Jane Applegate, "Don't Let a Global Deal Get Yanked," *Los Angeles Times*, April 2, 1993
2. Tracy Wilen, *Doing Business with Japanese Men,* Stonebridge Press, 1992

"Women thought that just working hard alone would get them ahead. That is not the case. You also have to know how to play corporate politics. Like going to lunch.

"In my office or in any office you'll find that men never miss lunch. They are always going to lunch. Walk around and see how many more women are having a sandwich at their desk. Law firms, banks, any big company.

"But think of the informal exchange of ideas and learning about other projects that takes place at lunch."

—Maryann Correnti

WHAT YOU WEAR MATTERS

"If you take off your jacket, you take off your power. So you should have your jacket on, period, because that is what is perceived as powerful.

"I don't think we want to be like men or to look like men. At the same time, you can't ignore the research that says that the woman who comes to work in a dress is perceived as less powerful than the woman in a suit. Right or wrong, good or bad, that's the way it is. That's the game."

— Pat Heim, Ph.D.[1]

"Pantsuits still have the stigma of manual work, because that's the kind of outfit you would wear if you were lifting or stretching. In a funny way, it's like the stigma of a short-sleeve shirt."

— Susan Bixler, President,
Professional Image Inc.[2]

1.Pat Heim, Ph.D., personal interview
2.Trish Donnally, "Dressing for the Office," *San Francisco Chronicle*, January 20, 1992

"After I started moving up in the bank, the former CEO came up to me, and said very emphatically, 'No flowers.' He's really tall, six feet plus, and he always comes up really close when he talks to you. I said, 'What do you mean?' He said, 'That dress. It's got to go. You can wear it on weekends, but not at work. In the business world, women don't wear flowers. I just went by W.A. King's, and there is a great gray suit in the window. I think you should buy it.'

"I thought, it's hundreds of dollars and a gray suit, no way. I went by and looked at it. Luckily they didn't have my size. I told him they didn't have my size. He said, 'You need a gray suit. Bankers wear gray and navy blue.' So finally I bought a navy suit.

"He was really very supportive, mentoring. He would always say, 'What would you like to do? What sort of training would you like to be doing?' He'd give me books from Helen Gurley Brown and self-help books for women and say, 'Read this, it's good.'"

—*Lauri Leighty*

"I was at a meeting yesterday with two guys from New York in their pinstripe suits. We were discussing the new layout for the business page. One of the guys said, 'Well, the art and photographs on the page aren't that important because what are you going to take pictures of?'

"I said, 'I disagree with that completely. I think my page ought to look as good as the feature page. I'm not going to just take pictures of two white guys in pinstripe suits.'

'I'm really stricken by that putdown,' one of the guys said, 'particularly coming from a woman in a red jacket.'

"And it was true. I looked at me, and I looked at the other woman in the meeting, and we were both in red blazers. Like I have on a bright-colored, tailored jacket: pay attention to me. We were just as stereotypical as they were."

—*Cissy Ross*

❝I remember going down to a convention just to see what 500 executive women would look like. They looked like men. Even me.❞

—Terry Walker

❝I felt like I was playing a charade. You can put on a suit, go to work, know the language, say the latest buzz words, know how to play the game, look like you fit in, and you may not feel that way inside. People looked at me one way, but I knew I was really another person.❞

—Jan Hill

❝I kind of went through the trend of wearing the dowdy suit and the MBA bow tie and the hair pulled back and glasses. I really didn't like myself very well, and I got ignored anyway.

"I finally said the heck with that. I decided I had to be me. I started wearing high heels and silk dresses, wearing my hair down instead of a bun, and wearing makeup again. It had a very positive influence. I was certainly happier about myself, and I think I probably did a better job because of it.❞

—Sarah Litton

“ “**M**y company is run by white males who play golf or tennis. I don't play tennis. And I have no interest in golf.

"For a while I thought I should feign an interest in it because it would help me get ahead. But I thought, I'm just not that much of a hypocrite. I'm a good sport, and I'll go out if someone really wants me to play golf, as long as I don't irritate them to death because I'm so bad at it.

"But I do not want to spend 6 or 8 hours of my weekend doing that. I want to be with my family. That's just not my idea of a great way to spend a weekend. It's not that great an exercise. I figure I'll wait until I'm old, and then I'll do it. ” ”

—Donna Bates

“ “**I**'m putting together a women's golf clinic. I figure, men take all the time to do the "PD" thing, the personal development thing and take off on a Friday afternoon to play golf. What do women do? We can't say we're going shopping with a client. ” ”

—Cynthia Morris

❝I was never part of the informal social stuff that goes on in corporations. I was never a part of anybody's club: the golf thing or the poker game. I wasn't one of the boys.

"If there was a criticism that every single employer would have had of me, it was that I wasn't a team player. I felt much more oriented toward the success of the business as defined by the bottom line, did it make money or didn't it. Who felt good about whom, the harmony of the team didn't seem very important. But those things are important to the corporation.

"Esprit de corps and rapport are all important to build a team that you trust. There is nothing wrong with management trying to build those kinds of relations between people. But it doesn't seem easy to build that across gender. And corporations have put things in place, like golf outings, that don't really facilitate those kinds of connections between men and women. For right now, I don't think women can be part of the corporate team.❞

—Gail Seneca

THE TEN LEADING OCCUPATIONS OF WORKING WOMEN

1870, 1970, 1993

	1870	1970	1993
1.	Domestic Servants	Secretaries	Secretaries
2.	Agricultural Laborers	Retail Sales	Retail Sales
3.	Tailoresses & Seamstresses	Bookkeepers	Food Preparers and Servers
4.	Milliners, Dress & Mantua* Makers	Elementary School Teachers	Elementary School Teachers
5.	Teachers (Not Specified)	Typists	Registered Nurses
6.	Cotton-mill Operators	Waitresses	Bookkeepers
7.	Laundresses	Sewers and Stitchers	Nurses' Aides
8.	Woolen-mill Operators	Registered Nurses	Information Clerks
9.	Farmers and Planters	Cashiers	Adjusters and Investigators (Insurance, Billing, etc.)
10.	Nurses	Private Household Cleaners and Servants [1]	Sales Supervisors and Proprietors

* A cloak formerly worn by women

---

1. Decennial Census, 1870-1940; U.S. Women's Bureau, "Occupations of Women, 1950, 1960, and 1970," and U.S. Bureau of Labor Statistics for 1993 data

I BITE MY TONGUE A LOT

Modern Business: The Selected Writings of Elbert Hubbard

Elbert Hubbard, 1922

Selling Typewriters

"The Remingtons could not sell their machines [typewriters] unless they supplied an operator; and so they inaugurated a special branch of their business to educate women in business methods and to use the typewriter."

❝This is one of those companies where the stereotype of the white male business is alive and well. We have a very small percentage of women. The majority of women are not in upper level management at all, anywhere. We have one vice-president, and, as all the men are eager to point out, she does not have a staff. It is clearly a position that was created so they could say, we have a woman vice-president.

"I'm a single mom, I have been here for ten years. I'm here because it's secure income. But I bite my tongue a lot. It's not easy.❞

—Martha Conners

PROGRESS IS TOO SLOW

A 1992 survey of 400 top women executives in the nation's 1500 largest companies:

96% believe the pace of progress for women in corporate America is too slow.[1]

THE COMFORT FACTOR

78% of women in a *Working Woman* survey thought "comfort factor" was the top tendency for male executives to choose people like themselves for leadership roles [2]

GORDON CONFERENCE ON MOLECULAR GENETICS

"In 1988 I ran a Gordon Conference on molecular genetics which was funded by NIH. About 33 percent of the speakers and 45 percent of the attendees were women. Two years later, another conference on the same topic was arranged by some of my male colleagues. And only two of the speakers were women. I don't think you can attribute this to anything but an unconscious bias. In the biological sciences, there has been a tendency to think that we are doing so well that the problem is over. And most women would like to believe this. I believed it. but that is nonsense."

— Shirley Tilghman, molecular biologist, Princeton University [3]

---

1. Survey by Korn/Ferry International and UCLA's John E. Anderson Graduate School of Management
2. Survey reported in Basia Hellwig, "Who Succeeds and Who Doesn't," *Working Woman,* November 1991
3. Virginia Morell, "Speaking Out," *Science,* March 13, 1992

"I think the diversity problem can be described by what an officer at a corporation I worked for said when there were eighteen officers, fifteen white males, two men of color, and me. He was one of the white males. I was talking about the whole thing about hiring the best candidate for the job. He said, 'You know, there is never a single best candidate. What I always do is narrow the pool of qualified candidates down to the top two or three. And then I pick the person most like me.'"

—*Diana Peterson-More*

"There was a male vice-president who I thought was taking shots at me. I couldn't understand why because I'd never had a confrontation with him. We'd never had any harsh words. All I ever did was my job.

"I talked to a psychologist who knew both of us and he said, 'It's very simple. He thinks he should control everything that happens in his whole area. You work in that area. Every time you don't clear things with him, he takes it as personal insult and retaliates.'

"When I learned that, I regularly met with him. Women have the very naive view that, if you work hard, diligently, sincerely, that is going to be enough. I thought I had very pure motives in what I was doing, but the fact is that a very powerful person did not appreciate it and attached negative motives to it."

—Karen Thompson

"Before I realized the difference in the way men and women communicated, I would sit down with a partner to discuss a project and he would start either picking up the phone or doing something else because he didn't see where the conversation was going.

"Some of the men here are more linear than others. Now I know which ones to go into and say, 'I've got five points, a, b., etc.' They are comfortable with that.

"Women on the whole don't do it that way. They are all over the board discussing it. By the end of the conversation you've pretty much covered it all but not necessarily in a linear order.

"If women started realizing these differences in communication they might understand when they feel they are being discriminated against, it's not really a matter of discrimination because she's a woman, but because the communication is coming at the men in a way they don't know how to deal with.

"So they stop dealing with you, not because they don't like you as a woman, and they will be adamant to say that they have no problem with men and women. They just want you to think like they think!"

—*Lani Meanley Collins*

MEETINGS - GETTING HEARD

- Plunk yourself down in the middle of the conference table: don't sit meekly at the end where you'll be easy to ignore.
- Practice what you want to say to a friend or partner in advance. Allow yourself time to hone the language and develop the confidence you need to demand attention.
- Don't say in advance what you have to offer may not be to the point, make sense or really answer the question.
- Hit your central point first, and hit it hard. Women are faulted for adding too many personal details and not getting to the lead quickly enough — a style that causes men to tune out.
- Don't let your statements end with a question mark; speak in declarative sentences. Women's voices frequently lack a sense of conviction. If you don't feel confident, pretend that you do.
- Be someone who really listens so you aren't just waiting your turn to speak. Then you can be the one to take two or three ideas and clarify them, instead of, as so frequently happens, losing out to a man who says the same thing you said 20 minutes ago — when nobody was listening.[1]

---

1. Patricia O'Brien, "Why Men Don't Listen," *Working Woman*, February 1993

"You can be in a meeting with all men, and you're trying to express a point of view, and they'll come in and talk right over you.

"It's like they're not even recognizing that you're there. They may be hearing you, because sometimes they'll express the same thing that you've said without recognizing that you said it."

—Ella Kaye

"I got the feeling that I was invisible. I'd wonder, am I stupid, am I crazy, am I from Mars. I'd say something and there would be these blank looks. It was because it was a little different, it might be challenging, it might be something they weren't ready to hear. And boy, they didn't hear it. Then if one of them would turn that same phrase around somewhat differently, within minutes it would be a great idea."

—Diana Peterson-More

❝I tell women in the business world today, you want to be liked and respected, but if you can't have both, respected is far more important than liked.❞

—*Barbara Abrams Mintzer*

❝When you are working at a high level, you are in an environment that sooner or later is going to turn on you. And it's not just women. Men and women, when you reach upper levels, tend to be quite isolated.

"I would say that none of my superiors have a single friend in their environment. It's not really hostile, just wary. They'll be very polite, cordial, jokes, backslapping, but it's very lonely.

"You have to have an antidote to loneliness somewhere else in your lives because otherwise it's going to be very difficult. And I think many women take that harder than men do.

"Don't expect the office to fulfill emotional needs. It is an achievement place. You have to make provisions in your life to have your emotional needs satisfied elsewhere.❞

—*Joan Engstrom*

66 Just before our annual partners meeting, the chairman had a separate dinner just for the women partners. Afterwards, he had the company's Women's Issues Task Force give a presentation on what they were doing.

"I always thought I was one of the most radical people I knew. I walked out of there kind of laughing. A lot of my male partners asked how it went. I said, 'You're going to love this. Guess what, I'm one of the moderates.' They said, 'Oh, no, that is scary.' 99

—*Sarah Litton*

EMPLOYEES' IDEAS COUNT

200,000 companies in America employ 50 or more people

6,000 operate suggestion systems

1,000 are members of the national suggestion systems group

Estimates are that member organizations saved $2 billion in 1993 implementing 311,000 employee ideas. That is nearly double the savings for 1985.

EMPLOYEE SUGGESTIONS

Year	No. Suggestions	% Adopted	Savings
1985	1.33 million	25%	$1.3 bill
1986	1.24 million	26%	$1.8 bill
1987	1.02 million	24%	$2.0 bill
1988	1.01 million	29%	$2.2 bill
1989	.996 million	32%	$2.0 bill
1990	1.02 million	32%	$2.3 bill
1993*	.810 million	38%	$2.0 bill [1]

*In 1993 there were 3.3 million fewer employees in the organizations reporting than in 1990

1. Employee Involvement Association, Washington, D.C.

"One of our vice-presidents has been pushing for diversity for six years. He's very committed. It takes a long time. No effort is going to be managed from human resources, it has to be managed from the top. If there is not commitment from the top, it's not going to happen.

"It's becoming clear that direction from the top makes the difference, and the difference in the divisions is just startling. The vice president who supports diversity has one hundred percent mandatory diversity training for everybody in his group, and his division is phenomenally successful. He's responsible for tripling sales since he started the training. You can feel the energy in his division. Everybody wants to work there. People can't wait to post for jobs in his division. He absolutely demands valuing people."

—Karen Thompson

TOP TEN SOURCES OF STRESS ON THE JOB

1. Co-workers
2. Management policies
3. Paperwork
4. Financial problems
5. Lack of exercise
6. Customers
7. Communication problems
8. Personal problems
9. Competition
10. Rejection [1]

THE CORPORATE MILLSTONE

"During all the years working in corporations, I had a huge millstone around my neck so I had to walk stooped. Now that I don't have that and I have my own company, I can stand up and walk. It feels good. It's terrific not to have to contort yourself in order to just get by, to get along. Speaking frankly was something you didn't do in the corporate environment. It was very liberating to put the energy you have into productive things as opposed to diplomacy. I'm sure there is a value in diplomacy, but I'd rather spend my effort in productivity."

— Gail Seneca, Seneca Fund [2]

1. From a survey of readers of *Personal Selling Power*, March 1993
2. Gail Seneca, Managing Partner, Seneca Investment Fund, Personal interview

ENOUGH WAS ENOUGH

LABELS AND CAREER PATHS

"When I was growing up, social scientists maintained that men were 'instrumental' and 'task-oriented' whereas women were 'expressive' and 'person-oriented.' This was a fancier way of saying that men were best suited for work and women were best suited for motherhood. Experts explained that such division of emotion and physical labor was an ideal arrangement for family life, although, overall and if the truth be told, being expressive and person-oriented was not as healthy or desirable as being instrumental and task-oriented."

— Carol Tavris [1]

PERCENT OF WOMEN MANAGERS AROUND THE WORLD

43% of all management in the United States

40% of all management in Australia and Canada

8.3% of all management in Japan

4% of all management in Korea [2]

"All successful women I know have been broken-field runners. They go in one direction as far as they can, hit a wall and go in a different direction. The phrase 'career-path' has misled many people — male and female."

— Jane Bryant Quinn [3]

1. Carol Tavris, *The Mismeasure of Woman,* Simon & Schuster, 1992
2. Donna Jackson, "Shattering the Glass Ceiling," *New Woman,* September 1992
3. Maggie Mahar, "No Bull Advice," *Working Woman,* October 1992

“**I** was working for a company and I ran into one of those attitudes that since you're a female, you're not going to go anywhere.

"They were supposed to make me the office manager. I was working for two guys. I gave them a six page proposal of the way I'd set up the office: cost-justifications, budget allocations, how to make the changes that needed to be made.

"One of the men was really excited. He told me, 'Great proposal. Really well done.'

"He showed it to the other guy who called me into his office and said. 'It's a great proposal. Did you write that?' I said, 'Yes, I wrote it.' He said, 'The whole thing?' 'Yes, the whole thing,' I said, and he said, 'God, I could have sworn it was written by a professional.'

"I looked at him and I said, 'Dennis, it was written by a professional.' He said, 'No, that's not what I mean.' I said, 'I know exactly what you mean.' I left shortly after that. They hired a guy to do the computer things I was doing and another guy to be the office manager."

—*Lorraine Kennedy*

SELF-ESTEEM

Self-esteem protects people against the anxiety they'd otherwise experience from awareness of their vulnerability and — especially, mortality.

[Psychologists] boosted the self-esteem of a group of people by "testing" them and telling them what great personalities they had. Then they showed vivid video images of death from a documentary, "Faces of Death."

So distressing were the images, in fact, that no woman would even sit through the study. Still, the self-esteem insulated men from anxiety in response to the film; the men also reported few negative feelings of any kind afterwards. By contrast, anxiety ran high among men not told first how wonderful they were.

The feeling of being of personal value reduces susceptibility to anxiety largely because it evokes feelings of safety and security that were first created by good parenting and, ideally, later reinforced by a just society.[1]

1. Jeff Greenberg, Ph.D., University of Arizona in study reported in *Journal of Personality and Social Psychology*, Vol. 63, No.6

66The president of a company I used to work for is a real male chauvinist. He's into power and acts out a lot. The strong people move on. The others get into the mold, 'Well, I guess there must be something wrong with me. I have to put up with it because I won't get anything better.'

"And the company pays very well, so it keeps people with golden handcuffs. Some women I thought had great potential stayed too long, and now, in my opinion, they are dysfunctional. It's really sad.99

—Sari Weiner

DROPPING OUT

ACCOUNTING

46% of staffers in Big Six accounting firms are women.

4.9% of partners in Big Six accounting firms are women.

-27% membership decrease between 1981 and 1991 in American Women's Society of CPAs, from 4,507 to 3,300.[1]

LAW

In a survey of about 1,000 associates in nine midsize and large Manhattan firms comparing listings in 1986 and 1991:

72% of women had left their firms.

56% of men had left their firms.

8% of women had become partners.

21% of men had become partners.

"Among the women lawyers I know, the stresses of practice are not only bearable but acceptable if you feel what you're doing is — important."

— Harriet Rabb, professor, Columbia Law School [2]

1. *Accounting Today* Survey in "Why Accounting Doesn't Add Up," *Working Woman,* January 1993

2. Laura Mansnerus, "Why Women Are Leaving the Law," *Working Woman,* April 1993

66 **I** was compensation manager for a large
privately held company of 8,000 employees.
I made a presentation to the board of directors on
my first big project, our merit plan for the year.
They decided they would approve the plan during
the meeting and invited me to stay. I was on cloud
nine.

"There was one other woman in the room, the
director of marketing. I remember this so vividly
because it was a major turning point for me. She
was at the table, and I was sitting up against the
wall.

"The board was talking about a legal issue that
had come up around an EEO charge about
discrimination. One of the brothers who owned
the company turned to the other and said, 'We'll
have to do whatever we have to do here. We'll pay
them off. But I'll be damned if I'll ever have to
take a woman on the board of directors.'

I had been sitting there feeling so good. I
looked at this other woman who was stone-faced,
not reacting. I thought, 'I can't react. If I say
anything, I'll be fired.' So I waited out the
meeting, left the room, and started looking for
another job. 99

—*Jane Crane*

"Essentially it's a bunch of little things causing the top women to leave. I describe it as the water drip torture test. One drip doesn't bother you. It's the constant drip on your forehead that finally gets to you.

"I don't think many women understand it's the water drip torture driving them nuts: nobody paying attention to them in meetings, men making jokes that are demeaning toward women but not necessarily significant enough to make noise about, and other behavior like that.

"Most often women don't say I'm leaving because you guys drove me crazy. They say it's because I want more time with my family. Or I want a different life style. I think that's one of the things that's confusing for organizations. They don't get the kind of feedback that would be helpful for them to understand what's causing women to leave."

—Pat Heim

" A few years ago I was asked to look into why women left pharmaceuticals so much. No one had gathered that information because people who leave very rarely state the real reason. They don't burn bridges. In our system, the reason usually given is 'family obligations.'

"I went around talking to the people who knew the women who had left the company because of 'family obligation' and found out what they were doing. In every single case, there wasn't one person who had left and not gone to work some place else. How do you call that family obligation? You have to wonder what the family obligation was that took them right straight into another job.

"That experience made me acknowledge what I had refused to acknowledge before, at least consciously. I could see that one didn't succeed by hard work and keeping her mouth shut, that there was a lot more to it than that. And that there were some built-in advantages for part of the population; things just didn't happen for women no matter what they did. "

—*Elaine Mahla*

TALKING POWER

"Men's language is the language of the powerful. It is meant to be direct, clear, succinct, as would be expected of those who need not fear giving offense. It is the language of people who are in charge of making observable changes in the real world. Women's language developed as a way of surviving and even flourishing without control over economic, physical, or social reality. Then it is necessary to listen more than speak, agree more than confront, be delicate, be indirect, say dangerous things in such a way that their impact will be felt after the speaker is out of range of the hearer's retaliation."

— Robin Lakoff [1]

1. Robin Lakoff, *Talking Power: The Politics of Language*, Basic Books, 1990

"I got caught in the middle of a pissing contest. The VP of my division wanted to bring me back East and put me in advertising. I was blown away. Everything centers around advertising at that company. There are only one or two VPs who have made it through sales. I decided to go for it and sold my house.

"The national sales manager was very upset the VP usurped him. He wanted me stay in California to keep him looking good. Pretty soon I heard through the grapevine that the sales manager and the VP were negotiating where I was going to be working.

"When I heard that, I decided I had it with little men in gray suits, white button-down shirts, and red ties. I resigned.

"They tried to persuade me to stay. The national sales manager was shocked. I told him, 'You treated me like shit and I'm not going to take it from you or anybody.'

"Leaving his office, I said, 'You know, I could have prevented all this. I could have looked at you and put on the coy routine that so many women do and said, Oh, I don't know how this got so out of control and I really need your help. Will you please help me?'

"He gave me a sidelong look and said, 'You're right.'"

—*Jan Hill*

WHO'S YOUR MENTOR

49% of women interviewed had male mentors.

19% of women interviewed had female mentors.

32% of women interviewed had both.[1]

"Salt and pepper matchups work best. To seek a mentor who is merely a more experienced clone of yourself has dubious value. Instead, find someone who has a different style, different values, a different philosophy — this enriches a younger person's growth.

"Don't use your mentor like a crutch. A mentor can become a crutch — and this violates the intent of the relationship. When I hear about people scheduling emergency meetings with their mentors — or calling them at 5 a.m. — then I know that the contract has been broken."

— Dr. Thomas L. Brown [2]

"It's important that more women in senior positions take the responsibility of mentoring other women. Women in America are still a generation away from success, and we need to build a network."

— Carol Bartz, CEO, Autodesk [3]

1. A survey done by Joan D. Jeruchim and Pat Shapiro, "Women, Mentors, and Success," 1992 in Alexandra Siegel, "Making the Most of Mentors: Yours Differ from His," *Working Woman*, May 1992

2. Dr. Thomas L. Brown, "Match Up With A Mentor," *Industry Week*, October, 1990

3. "Growing More High-Tech Women," *PC Magazine*, February 23, 1993

MENTORS AND ROLE MODELS

MENTORING BASICS

HOW TO FIND ONE

In most cases mentoring happens fairly naturally. You work with someone and find you have good communication and just sort of click. Then you go to them and seek career advice.

If the woman is looking for mentoring, she can initiate it by sitting down with someone she's worked with and has a good relationship with and saying, "I'd like to get some career advice from you." Don't say, I want you to be my mentor. A lot of people don't understand what that really means.

Typically you go to somebody who is at the next level up. Don't try to go too high. You are better off to go with your immediate level supervisor because that person is closer to what is going on.

THE MOST IMPORTANT THING YOU CAN LEARN

A lot of women haven't been as organizationally smart as men have.

Women tend to be very project oriented and think if they do a good job, that is all it takes. It takes more than just being able to roll up your sleeves and crunch the work out yourself. You have to be able to manage people, manage projects. That's where you need the help of somebody who knows what to do.

— Shirley Cheramy[1]

1. Shirley Cheramy, Managing Partner, Price, Waterhouse, Los Angeles. Personal interview with the editor

66"The first advice I'd give a woman starting out is to attach herself to a star. Get a mentor and make sure the relationship will bring you rewards. And be sure to look for the person who not only wants to get the work out of you but wants to develop you too."

—Rosemary S. Whitney

66"My first boss really gave me some good advice on how to get ahead and deal with the politics in the company. He said, 'Always call everyone by their first name, don't tell anyone you can type, and never get anyone coffee.'"

—Sandra Evers-Manly

MENTORING BASICS

GENDER IS A NON-ISSUE

I had a number of male mentors along the way. There weren't any female mentors because there weren't any females up there.

It doesn't matter if your mentor is the same gender. That's a non-issue. What you really want is somebody who is doing a good job, who's well respected within the organization, and who will take enough interest to talk to you.

Male or female, you can't succeed in any organization of any size without people in there pulling for you.

Ultimately a mentor, if they are really doing their job, is somebody who pounds on the table and says, "This is one of the best people we have. Give her this job or this promotion or whatever." They become a real advocate for the person.

MENTORS CHANGE

Over time your mentors change. In some cases you have more than one person you talk to and get help from. Because nothing is ever cut and dried, I think it helps to have different people that you talk to at different times. People come and go, and it helps to get different people participating in the process.

— Shirley Cheramy[1]

1. Shirley Cheramy, Managing Partner, Price, Waterhouse, Los Angeles. Personal interview with the editor

66**I** think many women aren't yet competent at dealing with power and resources. I think we don't know how to play the game.

"I'm very good at the politics. I've spread my mentorship around. I've always been just one away from the vice president and always working for one of the top management people. I have to go away from the office in order to meet with them, or the other women there get their noses out of joint.99

— *Beth North*

66**S** ometimes you have to be careful about mentors. Should that mentor leave the company, what tends to happen is all of a sudden you have nobody. That happened to me. People who came at the same time I did and had their advocates here were able to excel. It wasn't until after I decided to challenge how we promoted people, go after job after job, and ask why I didn't get it that I started to get equal opportunity. People shouldn't get a job just because of a mentor.99

— *Sandra Evers-Manly*

MENTORING BASICS

If you've got several mentors, don't get them together in a group. "That wouldn't be much fun. When you are trying to dispense wisdom, you don't want to compete for airtime."

— Leonard Schlesinger, associate professor,
Harvard's Graduate School of Business
Administration

HOW TO PICK A MENTOR AND MAKE IT WORK

- Is that person ready to share? People who have reached a certain level of material success get personal satisfaction from seeing others succeed.
- Can the person understand your business? If you are an entrepreneur, a surgeon probably isn't the best mentor.
- Does the person have credibility?
- Will the person share your values?
- Shut up and let the mentors do the talking. Show your seriousness about listening by actually implementing some of the ideas you hear.
- Pay promptly. Not in money, of course, but in gratitude and feedback. "There have been a number of times when they have gone different routes from those I suggested. But they'll call and say, 'We just wanted you to know we did it this way, but we still appreciate your input.'"

— Russell Epker, venture capitalist [1]

---

1. Joshua Hyatt, "Words from the Wise," *Inc.*, June 1991

66 **A**ll our board members think they are responsible for my success. They all think that they are the mentor who has made me what I am today.

"My style is really warm and friendly, so it's very common when we have meetings and I haven't seen a board member for a while, we always hug and kiss. They all feel that I'm their daughter who's done well. We have one woman director, and I think she was the one who started it. Then all the directors started doing that.

"The first time a new member saw that, he almost died. His mouth just dropped open. 99

—Lauri Leighty

"I read a study that showed in schools, males are allowed to figure things out for themselves and females aren't. One of the results of this is women grow up accustomed to being mentored and assisted.

"Right after I read this research, I was in a class where we were being taught how to make materials for presentations. A man had a question about putting together a transparency. The instructor gave him a minimum amount of instruction and said, 'Figure it out.' A woman asked a question about her transparency. The instructor sighed, grabbed it out of her hands, did it himself, and gave it back to her.

"Information and helping someone succeed are very important forms of currency. Women don't recognize that. They just expect it will automatically come to them.

"In the male culture, if someone gives you advice, it's rare and it's a good deal. And you owe them and you better know that you owe them and be ready to pay it back. When a woman comes into the system and shows no sense of obligation, the man is pissed. It's like, 'Who does she think she is that she can just expect this?'

"Women need to show attending behavior when they're working with men. A lot of times I've heard, 'I told her that, and she didn't even get out her pad and write any notes. I won't teach her anything again.' A woman needs to make eye contact, listen, get out her pad of paper and write some notes, say thank you, and bring it up sometime later to show that you implemented what they told you. If you do that you'll get a lot more help. If you don't, they'll think you're someone who is arrogant and doesn't care, and you may never get help again."

—Cindy Webster

"Over the years I have helped a lot of women in their upward mobility, whether it be helping them rewrite their resumes or talking with them and advising them on the kind of educational courses to take.

"At least half of them act like they don't know you after they've gotten to where they want to be. That's a more recent phenomenon.

"I keep thinking, here I am, helping people right and left, and I ain't getting any strokes for it. Why aren't they grateful?"

—*Patricia Montemayor*

ROLE MODEL SHORTAGE

WHITE MALES ARE:

39% of the population

70% of tenured college faculty

77% of Congress

77% of TV news directors

82% of Forbes 400 (worth at least $265 million)

90% of daily newspaper editors

92% of state governors [1]

WOMEN IN THE MEDIA 1993

In a survey of done by Women, Men & Media Project, women were referred to only 13% of the time in 20 newspapers. The survey looked at front page, first page of local section and the op-ed page.

TV Network News:

86% of stories were reported by men

79% of on-camera commentary showed men

20% interviewed on nightly news were women

14% of network correspondents were women [2]

1. David Gates, "White Male Paranoia," *Newsweek*, March 29, 1993
2. Study done for Women, Men and Media Project, "News Still a Man's World, Annual Media Survey Reveals," Associated Press, April 7, 1993

"When women are unfair, usually it's because they've had a male role model and they are doing the same thing the men did.

"You see it in supervisory roles. There are these characteristics that we call male, which are typically unsympathetic, uncaring, and autocratic. When you see that in a woman, you get the impression she's just trying to be one of the men.**"**

—Leila Srour

"Typically men have controlled women in traditional jobs by pitting them against one another. Looking back when I was a young lawyer, we had four young women lawyers, and we were all pitted against one another. The idea is only one or two of you is going to be anything, and it's up to you to fight it out. So we felt very competitive.

"It has taken us 10 to 12 years to be friendly colleagues and support one another. So what I'm saying is you can be in a situation where you appear to have a peer group when you don't.**"**

—Karen Thompson

NO ONE EVER TOLD ME I COULD

"When I graduated from college, my only choice was get married, be a nurse or a teacher. After I had my children and was in graduate school, I took an aptitude test and found I was in the 99th percentile in mechanical engineering. No one ever told me I could be a mechanical engineer."

— Maryann Battistini, Merrillville, Indiana
High School Counselor [1]

THE COMPUTER EXPERT EQUITY PROJECT

(A program training educators to reinforce girls' interest in math, science, and computer science.)

"The impact has been staggering. In Nebraska, the pre-calculus enrollment in one school had been 20 percent female and is now 45 percent. Female enrollment in technology education has multiplied four-fold over the last years in an Oklahoma school. In an Ohio school, girls using computers have increased from 25 percent to 50 percent."

— Jo Sanders, director of the Computer Equity
Expert Project [2]

1. Erin Kennedy, "Bias in classroom hold back women," Knight-Ridder News Service, December 27, 1993
2. Don Oldenburg, "The Message Behind the Gender Gap in Computer Training," *Washington Post*, April 26, 1993

"I'm the first woman partner in my group, and since there are a lot of women in the group who never had a chance to have women mentors or role models, I thought it might be helpful for the women to have some sort of a get-together to open the lines of communications.

"There was a lot of concern among the men that it could be viewed as fostering a gripe session. The men do not want admit that there is any kind of discrimination or any kind of difference in professional behavior. They do not want us raising concerns or making it appear that there is a problem. Like talking about it would make it worse.

"I don't think that's true. I think talking about it makes people a little bit cooler. There is very little that is as devastating as keeping it inside when you are ticked off at somebody."

—Sarah Litton

WOMEN MANAGERS

50% of entry-level management positions

25% of middle management positions

50% of officers and managers of 50 largest banks [1]

A 1992 SURVEY OF EXECUTIVE WOMEN

A survey of 400 top women executives in the nation's 1500 largest companies:

9% of women were executive vice presidents

23% of women were senior vice presidents [2]

Today's Fortune 500 will not resemble the [list in] 2002. Today's senior executives will retire in the 1990s. Just below them is a cadre of female talent age 35-45 that will break into CEO and senior executive positions by decade's end.

"If you look at the ranks of any major corporation below the top 20 people you'll find that 50 percent of the next group of managers are women."

— Lester Korn, president,
Korn/Ferry International [3]

---

1. Naomi Wolf, "The Beauty Myth," William Morrow and Co., 1991
2. Survey done by Korn/Ferry International and UCLA's John E. Anderson Graduate School of Management
3. Patricia Aburdene and John Naisbitt, "Megatrends for Women," Villard Books, 1992

WOMEN ON MANAGING

JAPAN'S LABOR SHORTAGE

"The labor shortage is so bad that we are actually having to use women for their brainpower instead of hiring them for their looks."

— A recruiter for Japan's Asahi National Broadcasting Company [1]

IN AMERICA

- Nearly 60% of all women work
- 3 out of 5 new workers in the next decade will be women
- An estimated 66 million women will be working in the year 2000.[2]

JENNIE JONES' POEM

"Perhaps you're not sure if I'm worth renewing,
Perhaps there's talking where there should be doing.
Perhaps this decision which looms so large,
Might already be made, were a woman in charge." *[3]

*A fax Jennie Jones sent to the men trying to decide whether or not to renew her talk show

1. *New Woman*, September 1992
2. 9to5 Profile of Working Women, 1992-1993 edition
3. *TV Guide*, March 30, 1993

KATE SILSBURY: I have to be much more firm with male employees. They don't listen to me if I don't tell them they have to do something rather than just giving them friendly helpful coaching. Women like you to make suggestions. Women like to make suggestions to each other and coach each other in a friendly way.

SHELLEY BOOKSPAN: I haven't noticed it. Maybe I'm more dictatorial.

CATHERINE DISHION: I don't honestly think you can deal on an emotional basis with a man just because they are different. They say things to each other and don't take it personal. I think that's why we have to deal a little differently with men versus women.

I've always tried to be the very best boss I could possibly be because I have seen a lot of very bad male bosses. I'm not saying there aren't a lot of bad female bosses. I definitely do not tell my employees what to do. I suggest that they do this.

NANCY HAWKS: I think that is an innate feminine quality in this culture. We women are the supporters, the doers, the nurturers, the caretakers. It is very difficult for us to tell someone to do something for us. I hated it when I had to do it.

LOUISE RAMSEY: My experience is a little bit different. I worked in a corporation in upper management before I started my own business. I worked directly with men all the time. I loved it.

I always thought dealing with men was wonderful because it was real quick, easy and fast. You got to the point directly. There was always clear communications. You always knew what was expected of you.

When I went back into a world where I was dealing more with women, it was very difficult. I had to learn how to talk all over again.

MARSHA BAILEY: I don't think being indirect is just a thing women do. I used to work at a company where the guy who ran it fired his secretary by sending her a letter while she was on vacation.

I remember the first time I had to tell employees they really did a terrible job on something. It happened to be two men. I felt really terrible, probably as bad as they did having to tell them they screwed up. Maybe that's what the difference is. I don't know if men feel that bad about it or not.

SHELLEY: Oh sure they would. They're people too.

CATHERINE: I feel like I have multiple personalities. I go home, and I'm mother to my son, a wife to my husband, and a daughter to my father.

Then I come to work and I'm the boss of a great team of employees. When I'm making collections, trying to get my money from people who aren't paying, I always say I'm the manager, not the owner. Usually when you talk to women you get less conflict. Men will try to intimidate you. I've had men yell at me on the phone. Owners can make concessions. Managers can't.

Sometimes its hard to keep all these roles straight. Sometimes it's hard to remember who I am.

SHELLEY: I'm not sensing that what women are experiencing is all that different from what men experience. I agree that you do have to put on different roles. Often I have to switch back and forth in the course of a conversation.

But I can tell when I hear some of my male employees on the phone whether they are talking to a researcher or talking to a client. Their voices are very different.

CATHERINE: I don't think men have to do so much switching. I honestly think that a man can just be a man no matter what the situation is.

NANCY: I totally agree with Cathy. I remember one time when I was still married, my husband came home from the office, walked into the kitchen, and said, 'Take a letter.' I said, 'What?' He was just being his male self.

THE CHANGING COMPANY

"The need for more productive use of capital, to allow for rising living standards, is the force behind downsizing. The trend has little to do with old-fashioned labor costs, which amount to only about 5% of total costs in business today — where computerized equipment and knowledge account for so much. . . .

"And smaller, specialized companies create opportunity in other ways. It's no accident that women executives head five of the specialized cable channels — Nick at Nite, USA, Discovery, American Movie Classics and Bravo — that have been taking audience from those classic big companies, the fading TV networks. All those women once worked for the networks but found their opportunities in smaller companies — away from stifling bureaucracy."

— James Flanigan [1]

"We know from research that the degree to which events boost self-esteem is a consequence of taking ownership for them. Men are socialized to promote themselves and their own success and lay claim to it. But women are socialized to share responsibility for positive events [with others]. So if something good happens, they say, 'I wasn't the only one responsible — we did it together.'"

— Alex Zautra, Ph.D., professor of clinical psychology, Arizona State University [2]

1. James Flanigan, "Start-up Firms Can Balance Downsizing, Creating Jobs," *Los Angeles Times*, February 14, 1993
2. Victoria Secunda, "Shine with Your Success," *New Woman*, April 1993

MEN AND
THE CHANGING COMPANY

WOMEN-OWNED BUSINESSES

NUMBER OF WOMEN-OWNED BUSINESSES
1982 - 1992

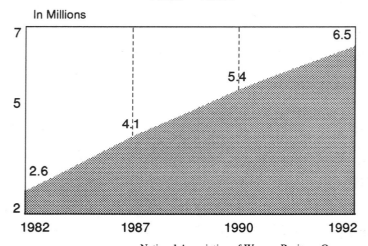

National Association of Women Business Owners

12 million people employed by women-owned businesses in 1992

11.7 million people employed by Fortune 500 companies in 1992 [1]

Women-owned businesses constitute one-third of the country's businesses, but account for only 13.9% of the gross receipts and are awarded only 1% of federal contracts.[2]

---

1. "Women Own a Larger Slice of American Corporations," *Los Angeles Times*, April 19, 1993
2. "Now, The Brick Wall," *Newsweek*, August 24, 1992

"We did an employee attitude survey. Everybody in the company filled it out, and we had it tabulated at the University. We had it cross-tabulated by full-time versus parttime, home office versus the retail store, and male versus female.

"Everything was above average. There are areas to work on, of course. But the odd thing was that the women rated the company even higher than men.

"Our consultant said he'd never seen that before. And I said, 'How many women-owned companies have you done this for?' He said, 'None.'"

—*Ann Jackson*

"Men live their whole lives in hierarchies. Everybody in the world is either above them or below them. On the other hand, women grow up in flat structures. There is never a boss dollplayer. If a woman is too bossy, she loses out. Girls negotiate differences rather than tell each other what to do.

"Not long ago, I was working with a group of middle managers, all men, in an aerospace firm that was trying to flatten out its organization. One of the things I brought up was self-managed teams. They were terrified of this.

'Who's going to do the performance appraisals? Who's going to determine the raises? You can't just let them determine raises!' they argued.

"I explained how a team can do its own performance appraisals, and you normally give them a pool of money and they negotiate that among themselves.

'You can't let them do that!' was the response.

"The next week I was working with a large company in the midwest. I was doing a gender-diversity thing. Again these were middle managers and all male. I again brought up the concept of self-managed teams. Again, they went berserk, like I was advocating total anarchy of the company.

"The week after that I conducted a workshop with middle managers in a hospital, all women nurses. For the heck of it I brought up the concept of self-managed teams. Their reaction was, that's very interesting. They thought it would be very helpful to them and went right into talking about how it could be used. No fear.

"That's when I began to realize that the changes that are happening in American business are really changes to women's ways, and the men are horrified because they are going to have to learn these new behaviors.**99**

—*Pat Heim*

THE CHANGING COMPANY

"Authority. . . is incompatible with persuasion, which presupposes equality and works through a process of argumentation. Where arguments are used, authority is left in abeyance. . . . The authoritarian relation between the one who commands and the one who obeys rests neither on common reason nor on the power of the one who commands; what they have in common is the hierarchy itself, whose rightness and legitimacy both recognize and where both have their predetermined stable place."

— Hanna Arendt [1]

"Knowledge and power. Power and knowledge. They circle one another like figures on a Greek vase. Now knowledge overtakes and transforms power. Now power gains momentum, engulfing knowledge. . . . The questions before us now are these: To what extent will the changing requirements of knowledge transform the conception and conduct of power relations in the informed organization? Or, will the deeply etched patterns of belief, behavior, and feeling associated with these power relations ultimately subvert the distribution of the new knowledge?"

— Shoshana Zuboff [2]

1. Hannah Arendt, "What Was Authority?" in Carl J. Friedrich, ed., *Authority*, Harvard University Press, 1958
2. Shoshana Zuboff, *In the Age of the Smart Machine*, Basic Books, 1988

" ❝ Some of the men we are hiring now, not ones who grew up with the company but those who got their experience somewhere else, go through culture shock when they come to our company. They see people as working for them, not with them.

"It's like, 'What do you mean, I can't just tell that person what to do?'

"We had a guy, a really bright guy who had two engineering degrees and an MBA from Harvard, a well-seasoned guy in his late 30s, we hired to supervise manufacturing. He just couldn't get the way we do things here.

"One day he walked into a clerical assistant's office and said, 'Sandy, Ann is shifting to this job and I need to have you pick up the work over here. This is the way we're going to do it.'

"She said, 'No thank you, I don't want it.' He went, 'Excuse me?'

"She said, 'I'm sorry, that isn't the job I hired on to do and it's not the kind of work I like to do and I'm not really interested.'

"The guy was shocked. He came into my office and said, 'I've got a problem. Sandy won't do this.'

"I said, 'You're right. You've got a problem. You need to find somebody who will.'

"He said, 'Can I replace her then?'

"I said, 'Absolutely not. She's doing the job she hired on for. We'll find another way of making it work.'

"He just didn't get it. He thought the people were supposed to do whatever you told them to whenever you told them to do it. The guy was totally out of place here.

"His name was Bob. Now we're bringing in a wonderful person to supervise the manufacturing. I know he'll just fit right in. But his name is Bob too. Some of the people asked if he couldn't be called something else."

—Kathy Odell

"The Seattle office landed a major new client, and another woman and I both, independent of each other, volunteered to work on that client, as did others. We were both selected.

"The client said to the partner in charge of selection, 'Bob, why is it that I have two women working on my audit?'

"He said, 'Fred, I wanted to give you the two very best people that I've got.'"

—*Shirley Cheramy*

RESOURCES

Included below are the names and addresses of some resources for working women. There are associations of women in almost every profession. Look in *The Encyclopedia of Associations* at your local public library for the women's organization for your profession.

9to5, National Association of Working Women, 238 W. Wisconsin Avenue, Milwaukee, WI 53203. (414)274-0925

9to5 Toll-Free Job Survival Hotline: (800)522-0925

American Business Women's Association, 9100 Ward Parkway, Kansas City, MO 64114. (816)361-6621

California Women's Law Center, 6024 Wilshire Boulevard, Los Angeles, CA 90036. (213)935-4101

Families and Work Institute, 330 Seventh Avenue, New York, NY 10001. (212)465-2044

Institute for Women's Policy Research, 1400 20th Street, N.W., Suite 104, Washington, DC 20036. (202)785-5100

National Association of Female Executives, 127 W. 24 Street, New York, NY 10011. (212)645-0770

National Association of Women Business Owners, 600 S. Federal St., Suite 400, Chicago, IL 60605. (312)922-0465

Professional Secretaries International, 10502 New Ambassador Drive, Kansas City, MO 64153. (816)891-6600

Women's Bureau, U.S. Department of Labor, 200 Constitution Ave, N.W., Washington, D.C. 20210. (202)219-6593

Women Employed, 22 W. Monroe, Suite 1400, Chicago, IL 60603. (312)782-5249

Women in Management, 2 N. Riverside Plaza, Suite 2400, Chicago, IL 60606. (312)263-3636

ALSO AVAILABLE FROM
BLUE POINT BOOKS

"Nobody ever told me when I had a baby and a job I'd have to go two years without sleep."

TWO YEARS WITHOUT SLEEP

Working Moms Talk About
Having a Baby and a Job

Edited by Cathy Feldman

Two Years Without Sleep, the first in Cathy Feldman's series of books based on her interviews with working women, brings you the experiences of working moms in their own words.

The book combines funny, moving, perceptive quotes, facts, advice from experts, and illustrations in an easy to read format.

Two Years Without Sleep starts with "Telling the Boss You're Pregnant" and ends with "Making It Work." Women love it, and men say its full of things they never understood before.

TWO YEARS WITHOUT SLEEP
ISBN 1-883423-01-5

Companies are using Blue Point Books' publications in their maternity and diversity programs, and community organizations are finding the books effective for both their educational programs and fund raising. For information about purchasing the books in quantity for your company or organization, please contract:

Blue Point Books
P.O. Box 91347
Santa Barbara, CA 93109-1347
(805)965-2635

BPB
Blue Point Books